Winning Well

Katie Peters

GRL Consultants,
Diane Craig and Monica Marx,
Certified Literacy Specialists

Pull Ahead READERS People Smarts

Lerner Publications ◆ Minneapolis

Note from a GRL Consultant
This Pull Ahead leveled book has been carefully designed for beginning readers. A team of guided reading literacy experts has reviewed and leveled the book to ensure readers pull ahead and experience success.

Lerner Publications Company
An imprint of Lerner Publishing Group, Inc.
241 First Avenue North
Minneapolis, MN 55401 USA

For reading levels and more information, look up this title at www.lernerbooks.com.

Main body text set in Memphis Pro 24/39
Typeface provided by Linotype

Photo Acknowledgments
The images in this book are used with the permission of: © andresr/Getty Images, pp. 8–9; © FatCamera/Getty Images, pp. 10–11, 14–15, 16 (center); © LightFieldStudios/Getty Images, p. 3; © Morsa Images/Getty Images, pp. 12–13, 16 (left); © ViewStock/Getty Images, pp. 6–7, 16 (right); © vladans/Getty Images, pp. 4–5.

Front cover: © FatCamera/Getty Images.

Library of Congress Cataloging-in-Publication Data

Names: Peters, Katie, author.
Title: Winning well / Katie Peters.
Description: Lerner publications. | Minneapolis : Lerner Publications , 2022. | Series: Be a good sport. Pull ahead readers. People smarts. Nonfiction | Includes index. | Audience: Ages 4–7 | Audience: Grades K–1 | Summary: "Winning makes us feel good. But when we win, someone else loses. Learn how to be a good winner no matter what game you play. Pairs with the fiction title Good Game"— Provided by publisher.
Identifiers: LCCN 2021010376 (print) | LCCN 2021010377 (ebook) | ISBN 9781728440903 (library binding) | ISBN 9781728444420 (ebook)
Subjects: LCSH: Sportsmanship—Juvenile literature.
Classification: LCC GV706.3 .P466 2022 (print) | LCC GV706.3 (ebook) | DDC 175—dc23

LC record available at https://lccn.loc.gov/2021010376
LC ebook record available at https://lccn.loc.gov/2021010377

Manufactured in the United States of America
1 – CG – 12/15/21

Table of Contents

Winning Well

I won the game.

I tell my friend, "Good job."

I won the race.
I tell my friend,
"You ran fast too."

I won the match.
I tell my friend,
"You are a good player."

I won the race.
I tell my friend, "You
almost won that time."

I won the game.
I tell my friend,
"Thank you for playing."

It is fun to play with
my friends.
We are all good winners.

How do you show you are a good sport when you win?

Did You See It?

cards

goggles

net

Index